The Truths of God's Word

Diana Kleyn
Joel R. Beeke

Reformation Heritage Books
Grand Rapids, Michigan 49525
Christian Focus Publications
Fearn, Tain, Scotland, IV20 1TW

© copyright 2002 Reformation Heritage Books

ISBN # 1-892777-231

This book published in 2002 by
Reformation Heritage Books
2919 Leonard St., NE, Grand Rapids, MI 49525
Phone: 616-977-0599/ Fax: 616-285-3246
e-mail: RHBookstore@aol.com
website:www.heritagebooks.org
and
Christian Focus Publications
Geanies House, Fearn, Tain, Ross-shire,
IV201TW, Scotland, U.K.
email: info@christianfocus.com
website: www.christianfocus.com

Printed and bound by
Cox & Wyman, Reading, Berkshire

All scripture quotations are taken from the
King James Version of the Bible.

*For additional Reformed literature, both new and used,
request a free book list from the above addresses.*

FOREWORD

This simple summary of the truths of God's Word, compiled as a set of questions and answers, is aimed at helping children aged 7 to 9 to learn what everyone needs to know. The learning of doctrine is not salvation but a good foundation of truth is valuable. Knowing God's truths is the soil in which the seed of saving faith may grow and it combats false ideas that easily divert young minds.

The Truths of God's Word can be used at home, for catechism class, for home schooling, and in Christian schools. Teaching our children, however, is primarily our responsibility as parents. The church and Christian educators may assist us.

As you teach children, say with David, "Come, ye children, hearken unto me: I will teach you the fear of the LORD" (Ps. 34:11). Encourage them to plead upon God's own promise, "Those that seek me early shall find me" (Prov. 8:17b). And encourage yourself with Proverbs 22:6: "Train up a child in the way he should go: and when he is old, he will not depart from it."

A *Teachers' Manual for the Truths of God's Word* is available from Reformation Heritage Books, 2919 Leonard NE, Grand Rapids, MI 49525. (RHBookstore@aol.com) and Christian Focus Publications Geanies House, Fearn, Tain, Ross-shire, IV20 1TW, Scotland, UK. (Info@christianfocus.com)

CONTENTS

CHAPTER ONE

Who Is God?

1. Can we see God?

No, God cannot be seen for He is a spirit.

"God is a Spirit: and they that worship him must worship him in spirit and in truth" (John 4:24).

"Now the Lord is that Spirit: and where the Spirit of the Lord is, there is liberty" (2 Corinthians 3:17).

2. How many gods are there?

There is only one God, yet He is three Persons.

"But when the Comforter is come, whom I will send unto you from the Father, even the Spirit of truth, which proceedeth from the Father, he shall testify of me" (John 15:26).

"And Jesus, when he was baptized, went up straightway out of the water: and, lo, the heavens were opened unto him, and he saw the Spirit of God descending like a dove, and lighting upon him: and lo a voice from heaven, saying, This is my beloved Son, in whom I am well pleased" (Matthew 3:16-17).

3. Where is God?

God is everywhere at the same time.

> *"Can any hide himself in secret places that I shall not see him? saith the LORD. Do not I fill heaven and earth? saith the LORD"* (Jeremiah 23:24).

> *"Whither shall I go from thy spirit? or whither shall I flee from thy presence?"* (Psalm 139:7).

4. What does God know about you and me?

He knows everything we think, say, and do; He knows all things.

> *"For there is not a word in my tongue, but, lo, O LORD, thou knowest it altogether"* (Psalm 139:4).

> *"Neither is there any creature that is not manifest in his sight: but all things are naked and opened unto the eyes of him with whom we have to do"* (Hebrews 4:13).

5. Is God powerful?

God is almighty; He rules over heaven and earth and hell.

> *"The LORD hath prepared his throne in the heavens; and his kingdom ruleth over all"* (Psalm 103:19).

> *"For the LORD most high is terrible; he is a great King over all the earth"* (Psalm 47:2).

6. Does God ever break a promise?

No, for God is faithful.

"He is faithful that promised" (Hebrews 10:23b).

"Faithful is he that calleth you, who also will do it" (1 Thessalonians 5:24).

7. What is one of God's promises to children?

"I love them that love me; and those that seek me early shall find me" (Proverbs 8:17).

"But Jesus called them unto him, and said, Suffer little children to come unto me, and forbid them not: for of such is the kingdom of God" (Luke 18:16).

8. Is God good, even when bad things happen?

Yes, God never does evil. God is good to us in showing us His salvation, though we deserve no good at all.

"Good and upright is the LORD: therefore will he teach sinners in the way" (Psalm 25:8).

"Or despisest thou the riches of his goodness and forbearance and longsuffering; not knowing that the goodness of God leadeth thee to repentance?" (Romans 2:4).

9. Why does God have so many names?

Each of God's names tell us something about God and His greatness.

"Therefore my people shall know my name" (Isaiah 52:6a).

"Stand up and bless the LORD your God for ever and ever: and blessed be thy glorious name,

which is exalted above all blessing and praise"
(Nehemiah 9:5b).

10. *Where does God show us who He is?*
We learn who God is from nature, but especially from His Word, the Bible.

> *"The heavens declare his righteousness, and all the people see his glory"* (Psalm 97:6).

> *"Search the scriptures; for in them ye think ye have eternal life: and they are they which testify of me"* (John 5:39).

11. *How can we learn about God from nature?*
We can see God's power and majesty in the things He created.

> *"Of old hast thou laid the foundation of the earth: and the heavens are the work of thy hands"* (Psalm 102:25).

> *"Thou, even thou, art LORD alone; thou hast made heaven, the heaven of heavens, with all their host, the earth, and all things that are therein, the seas, and all that is therein, and thou preservest them all; and the host of heaven worshippeth thee"* (Nehemiah 9:6).

12. *Can we learn more about God from His Word?*
Yes, the Lord teaches us the way of salvation in the Bible.

> *"For I am not ashamed of the gospel of Christ: for it is the power of God unto salvation to every one that believeth; to the Jew first, and also to the Greek"* (Romans 1:16).

> *"And that from a child thou hast known the holy scriptures, which are able to make thee wise unto salvation through faith which is in Christ Jesus"* (2 Timothy 3:15).

13. Who wrote the Bible?

The Holy Spirit inspired some of God's servants long ago to write His words.

> *"All scripture is given by inspiration of God, and is profitable for doctrine, for reproof, for correction, for instruction in righteousness"* (2 Timothy 3:16).

> *"For the prophecy came not in old time by the will of man: but holy men of God spake as they were moved by the Holy Ghost"* (2 Peter 1:21).

14. Why is the Bible the most precious book in the world?

Because God speaks to us through His Word and tells us about the Lord Jesus Christ, the only way of salvation.

> *"And Jesus answered him, saying, It is written, That man shall not live by bread alone, but by every word of God"* (Luke 4:4).

> *"But these are written, that ye might believe that Jesus is the Christ, the Son of God; and that believing ye might have life through his name"* (John 20:31).

Questions to think about:

1. Are you happy that God knows all that you think, and say, and do?

2. Are you glad that God is stronger than sin, and Satan, and your sinful heart?

3. How should God's faithfulness encourage you to seek Him early?

4. Does it amaze you that such a great and holy God is willing to teach you so patiently all about Himself?

5. We are often unwilling to listen to God and His Word. Why should that make you sad and ashamed?

6. Do you pray to God about everything? Do you need Him for everything?

7. Do you believe that God can save you and that He is willing to save you? Is that your desire?

8. Why should the Bible be the most precious book in the world to you?

CHAPTER TWO

Who Are We?

1. *What was man like when God created him?*
He was perfect, for he was created in the image and likeness of God.

> *"So God created man in his own image, in the image of God created he him; male and female created he them"* (Genesis 1:27).

> *"And God saw every thing that he had made, and, behold, it was very good"* (Genesis 1:31a).

2. *Did man remain good, and obedient to God?*
No, he chose to obey Satan rather than God.

> *"And when the woman saw that the tree was good for food, and that it was pleasant to the eyes, and a tree to be desired to make one wise, she took of the fruit thereof, and did eat, and gave also unto her husband with her; and he did eat"* (Genesis 3:6).

> *"Know ye not, that to whom ye yield yourselves servants to obey, his servants ye are to whom ye obey; whether of sin unto death, or of obedience unto righteousness?"* (Romans 6:16).

3. *What was the result of Adam and Eve's disobedience in their fall in Eden?*

They became sinners, separated themselves from God, and died.

"But of the tree of the knowledge of good and evil, thou shalt not eat of it: for in the day that thou eatest thereof thou shalt surely die" (Genesis 2:17).

"But your iniquities have separated between you and your God, and your sins have hid his face from you, that he will not hear" (Isaiah 59:2).

4. *In what way did Adam and Eve die that day in the Garden?*
Even though their bodies did not die immediately, their love to God died, and so they died spiritually.

"The soul that sinneth, it shall die" (Ezekiel 18:20).

"For the wages of sin is death" (Romans 6:23a).

5. *But if Adam and Eve sinned, then why are we sinful too?*
Adam was the head of the human race, and thus his sinful nature was passed on to all his children.

"Wherefore, as by one man sin entered the world, and death by sin; and so death passed upon all men, for that all have sinned" (Romans 5:12).

"For as in Adam all die, even so in Christ shall all be made alive" (1 Corinthians 15:22).

6. *Are babies sinners, too, even though they have not committed any actual sins?*

Yes, they have original sin, or a sinful heart, passed on to them from Adam and Eve.

"Who can say, I have made my heart clean, I am pure from my sin?" (Proverbs 20:9).

"If we say that we have no sin, we deceive ourselves, and the truth is not in us" (1 John 1:8).

7. *Is this why we continually rebel against God?*
Yes; by nature we do not want God to rule over us, and we want to do our own will.

"The carnal mind is enmity against God" (Romans 8:7).

"The imagination of man's heart is evil from his youth" (Genesis 8:21b).

8. *Can we do any good at all?*
No, for in our fallen state we continue to sin in thought, word, and action.

"And God saw that the wickedness of man was great in the earth, and that every imagination of the thoughts of his heart was only evil continually" (Genesis 6:5).

"The heart is deceitful above all things, and desperately wicked: who can know it?" (Jeremiah 17:9).

Questions to think about:

1. Does it grieve you that by nature you are unwilling to serve God, who is so worthy of honor?

2. Has the Holy Spirit shown you that you are

incapable of doing any good, or do you think that you are not very sinful? Do you secretly think that the Bible is exaggerating about how wicked our hearts are?

3. What do you do after you have sinned? Do you try to forget about it, or do you confess it? Why is it always best to confess our sins?

4. Do you wish to serve God with your whole heart? Why is it important to begin serving the Lord while we are still young?

5. Do you think you would never have committed such a foolish sin as Adam and Eve did in Paradise?

CHAPTER THREE

Who Should We Be?

1. What does God require of each one of us?
He has commanded us to be perfect.

> *"Thou shalt be perfect with the LORD thy God"* (Deuteronomy 18:13).

> *"Let your heart therefore be perfect with the LORD our God, to walk in his statutes, and to keep his commandments, as at this day"* (1 Kings 8:61).

2. Does God give us any rules?
Yes, the Ten Commandments.

> *"And Moses called all Israel, and said unto them, Hear, O Israel, the statutes and judgments which I speak in your ears this day, that ye may learn them, and keep, and do them"* (Deuteronomy 5:1).

> *"Ye shall observe to do therefore as the LORD your God hath commanded you: ye shall not turn aside to the right hand nor to the left"* (Deuteronomy 5:32).

3. What is the summary of the law?
We must love God above all and our neighbor as ourselves.

"Jesus said unto him, Thou shalt love the Lord thy God with all thy heart, and with all thy soul, and with all thy mind. This is the first and great commandment. And the second is like unto it, Thou shalt love thy neighbour as thyself" (Matthew 22:37-39).

"And this commandment have we from him, That he who loveth God love his brother also" (1 John 4:21).

4. Where can we learn all that God requires of us?
In His holy Word.

"But be ye doers of the word, and not hearers only" (James 1:22).

"Ye shall diligently keep the commandments of the LORD your God, and his testimonies, and his statutes, which he hath commanded thee" (Deuteronomy 6:17).

5. What must be our greatest joy?
To glorify God, which means to honor God in all that we think, say, and do.

"Whether therefore ye eat, or drink, or whatsoever ye do, do all to the glory of God" (1 Corinthians 10:31).

"For ye are bought with a price: therefore glorify God in your body, and in your spirit, which are God's" (1 Corinthians 6:20).

6. Is God satisfied with half-hearted devotion?
No, we must love and trust Him completely at all times.

> *"Though he slay me, yet will I trust in him"* (Job 13:15).
>
> *"Trust in the LORD with all thine heart; and lean not unto thine own understanding"* (Proverbs 3:5).

7. *What does Jesus say about being kind?*

We must love those who hate us, as Jesus Himself did.

> *"But I say unto you, Love your enemies, bless them that curse you, do good to them that hate you, and pray for them which despitefully use you, and persecute you"* (Matthew 5:44).
>
> *"Be ye therefore merciful, as your Father also is merciful"* (Luke 6:36).

8. *What does Jesus teach about money and earthly things?*

The Lord Jesus must be more important to us than these things.

> *"But seek ye first the kingdom of God, and his righteousness; and all these things shall be added unto you"* (Matthew 6:33).
>
> *"For the kingdom of God is not meat and drink; but righteousness, and peace, and joy in the Holy Ghost"* (Romans 14:17).

9. *How did John the Baptist describe what we should be?*

John said, "He must increase, but I must decrease" (John 3:30).

> *"So foolish was I, and ignorant: I was as a beast*

before thee.... My flesh and my heart faileth: but God is the strength of my heart, and my portion for ever" (Psalm 73:22, 26).

10. *What did John mean when he said, "He must increase, but I must decrease"?*
He meant that we must love and honor Jesus Christ more and more, but become more and more disappointed in ourselves because of our sins.

> *"O wretched man that I am! who shall deliver me from the body of this death? I thank God through Jesus Christ our Lord"* (Romans 7:24-25a).

> *"Mortify therefore your members which are upon the earth"* (Colossians 3:5).

11. *Can we keep God's commandments perfectly and love Him as we should?*
No, for we have original and actual sin.

> *"Who can bring a clean thing out of an unclean? not one* (Job 14:4).

> *"For all have sinned, and come short of the glory of God"* (Romans 3:23).

12. *Does God excuse us then because we cannot serve Him perfectly?*
Not at all! God does not change, and neither did His laws and rules change because of our sin.

> *"The counsel of the LORD standeth for ever, the*

thoughts of his heart to all generations" (Psalm 33:11).

"But thou art the same, and thy years shall have no end" (Psalm 102:27).

Questions to think about:

1. Can we ever fully understand God and all His laws?

2. If we can't keep God's laws perfectly, does that mean we shouldn't try? Why should we try to obey God's laws?

3. Who has obeyed the law perfectly and what should that obedience teach us?

4. Do you love the Lord Jesus Christ, and wish to be like Him? Do you pray to be washed in His blood?

CHAPTER FOUR

How Can We Be What God Calls Us to Be?

1. *What was God's punishment to man for his disobedience in the garden of Eden?*
   Spiritual, physical, and eternal death.

   > *"Sin, when it is finished, bringeth forth death"* (James 1:15b).

   > *"For the wages of sin is death; but the gift of God is eternal life through Jesus Christ our Lord"* (Romans 6:23).

2. *Do we have any natural desires to seek after God?*
   No, "there is none that seeketh after God" (Romans 3:11b).

   > *"They are all gone aside, they are all together become filthy: there is none that doeth good, no, not one"* (Psalm 14:3).

3. *Is there then no hope for us?*
   Oh yes, there is! God has made a way for sinners to be saved.

   > *"Good and upright is the LORD: therefore will he teach sinners in the way"* (Psalm 25:8).

23

"This man receiveth sinners" (Luke 15:2b).

4. *Who is that way of salvation?*

The Lord Jesus Christ, who died on the cross and rose again from the dead.

> *"Jesus saith unto him, I am the way, the truth, and the life: no man cometh unto the Father, but by me"* (John 14:6).

> *"For God so loved the world, that he gave his only begotten Son, that whosoever believeth in him should not perish, but have everlasting life"* (John 3:16).

5. *Why did Jesus have to die?*

He died to pay for sins and to conquer death, so His people could be saved from spiritual and eternal death.

> *"For Christ also hath once suffered for sins, the just for the unjust, that he might bring us to God, being put to death in the flesh, but quickened by the Spirit"* (1 Peter 3:18).

> *"Wherefore Jesus also, that he might sanctify the people with his own blood, suffered without the gate"* (Hebrew 13:12).

6. *Why did Jesus have to suffer so terribly all through His life and especially at His death?*

Jesus had to bear God's wrath against sin so that He could be a perfect Savior.

> *"But he was wounded for our transgressions, he was bruised for our iniquities: the chastisement of*

our peace was upon him; and with his stripes we are healed" (Isaiah 53:5).

"The LORD hath laid on him the iniquity of us all" (Isaiah 53:6b).

7. *Jesus willingly suffered in the place of sinful people. Should that make us love Him with all our hearts?*
Yes, it should. May God break my hard heart and fill it with His love.

"I am the good shepherd: the good shepherd giveth his life for the sheep" (John 10:11).

"In this was manifested the love of God toward us, because that God sent his only begotten Son into the world, that we might live through him. Herein is love, not that we loved God, but that he loved us, and sent his Son to be the propitiation for our sins" (1 John 4: 9-10).

8. *How do we become one of God's children?*
The Holy Spirit gives us a new heart, turning us from sin, self, and Satan, and grants us faith in Jesus Christ. That makes us love and obey God.

"For by grace are ye saved through faith; and that not of yourselves: it is the gift of God" (Ephesians 2:8).

"Not by works of righteousness which we have done, but according to his mercy he saved us, by the washing of regeneration, and renewing of the Holy Ghost; which he shed on us abundantly through Jesus Christ our Saviour" (Titus 3:5-6).

9. *What must we do to be saved?*
We must repent and "believe on the Lord Jesus Christ" (Acts 16:31a).

> *"Repent ye and believe the gospel"* (Mark 1:15b).

> *"Jesus said unto her, I am the resurrection, and the life: he that believeth in me, though he were dead, yet shall he live"* (John 11:25).

10. *What other responsibilities do we have?*
We must pray earnestly, read God's Word with expectation, and go to church as often as we can, always asking God for His blessing.

> *"But this thing commanded I them, saying, Obey my voice, and I will be your God, and ye shall be my people: and walk ye in all the ways that I have commanded you, that it may be well unto you"* (Jeremiah 7:23).

> *"Not forsaking the assembling of ourselves together, as the manner of some is; but exhorting one another"* (Hebrews 10:25a).

11. *Why doesn't God save everybody?*
Because He is sovereign and does as He pleases.

> *"And all the inhabitants of the earth are reputed as nothing: and he doeth according to his will in the army of heaven, and among the inhabitants of the earth: and none can stay his hand, or say unto him, What doest thou?"* (Daniel 4:35).

> *"For he saith to Moses, I will have mercy on*

whom I will have mercy, and I will have compassion on whom I will have compassion. So then it is not of him that willeth, nor of him that runneth, but of God that sheweth mercy" (Romans 9:15-16).

12. Is this fair?

We deserve nothing but death, so we should be amazed that God saves anyone at all.

"Wilt thou also disannul my judgment? wilt thou condemn me, that thou mayest be righteous?" (Job 40:8).

"Nay but, O man, who art thou that repliest against God? Shall the thing formed say to him that formed it, Why hast thou made me thus? Hath not the potter power over the clay, of the same lump to make one vessel unto honour, and another unto dishonour?" (Romans 9:20-21).

Questions to think about:

1. Do you love God?

2. How do you feel when you read about Jesus' suffering and death?

3. Do you pray earnestly to God for a new heart?

4. Do you repent and believe the gospel?

5. Do you read God's Word often, hoping, praying, and expecting Him to speak to your heart?

6. When God speaks to your heart through His Word, do you answer like Samuel, "Speak, Lord, for thy servant heareth"?

7. Do you long to know more about God the Father, God the Son, and God the Holy Spirit?

6. Why should the Bible be an important part of your life? How sad would you be if you were forbidden to read God's Word?

CHAPTER FIVE

What the Triune God Does to Save Sinners

1. How many gods are there?
There is one God, but three Persons: God the Father, God the Son, and God the Holy Spirit.

> *"And Jesus, when he was baptized, went up straightway out of the water: and, lo, the heavens were opened unto him, and he saw the Spirit of God descending like a dove, and lighting upon him: and lo a voice from heaven, saying, This is my beloved Son, in whom I am well pleased"* (Matthew 3:16-17).

> *"But when the Comforter is come, whom I will send unto you from the Father, even the Spirit of truth, which proceedeth from the Father, he shall testify of me"* (John 15:26).

2. Can we ever understand this?
No, for we have limited minds and cannot understand everything about the Trinity.

> *"For my thoughts are not your thoughts, neither are your ways my ways, saith the LORD. For as the heavens are higher than the earth, so are*

*my ways higher than your ways, and my
thoughts than your thoughts*" (Isaiah 55:8-9).

"*Touching the Almighty, we cannot find him
out*" (Job 37:23a).

3. What does God the Father do for His children?
He provides everything necessary for soul
and body, and turns all things to their good.

"*And we know that all things work together for
good to them that love God, to them who are the
called according to his purpose*" (Romans 8:28).

"*Behold the fowls of the air: for they sow not,
neither do they reap, nor gather into barns; yet
your heavenly Father feedeth them. Are ye not
much better than they?*" (Matthew 6:26).

4. Does God the Father also care about the unconverted?
Yes, He earnestly calls them to turn to Him
and invites them to salvation.

"*Say unto them, As I live, saith the Lord GOD,
I have no pleasure in the death of the wicked; but
that the wicked turn from his way and live: turn
ye, turn ye from your evil ways; for why will ye
die, O house of Israel?*" (Ezekiel 33:11).

"*Ho, every one that thirsteth, come ye to the
waters, and he that hath no money; come ye, buy,
and eat; yea, come, buy wine and milk without
money and without price*" (Isaiah 55:1).

5. What is the providence of God?
God cares for His creation and governs all

things. All things happen by His fatherly hand, not by chance.

> *"The LORD is good to all: and his tender mercies are over all his works"* (Psalm 145:9).

> *"Are not two sparrows sold for a farthing? and one of them shall not fall to the ground without your Father. But the very hairs of your head are all numbered. Fear ye not therefore, ye are of more value than many sparrows"* (Matthew 10: 29-31).

6. *What does the name "Jesus" mean?*
Jehovah saves sinners.

> *"And she shall bring forth a son, and thou shalt call his name JESUS: for he shall save his people from their sins"* (Matthew 1:21).

> *"This is a faithful saying, and worthy of all acceptation, that Christ Jesus came into the world to save sinners; of whom I am chief"* (1 Timothy 1:15).

7. *Is Jesus the only way of salvation?*
Yes, for Acts 4:12 says, "Neither is there salvation in any other: for there is none other name under heaven given among men, whereby we must be saved."

> *"Jesus saith unto him, I am the way, the truth, and the life: no man cometh unto the Father, but by me"* (John 14:6).

8. *What does the name "Christ" mean?*
Anointed One.

"God anointed Jesus of Nazareth with the Holy Ghost and with power" (Acts 10:38a).

"Thou lovest righteousness, and hatest wickedness: therefore God, thy God, hath anointed thee with the oil of gladness above thy fellows" (Psalm 45:7).

9. To which offices was Christ anointed?
To the offices of prophet, priest, and king.

"The LORD thy God will raise up unto thee a Prophet from the midst of thee, of thy brethren, like unto me; unto him ye shall hearken" (Deuteronomy 18:15).

"Who his own self bare our sins in his own body on the tree, that we, being dead to sins, should live unto righteousness: by whose stripes ye were healed" (1 Peter 2:24).

"Unto him that loved us, and washed us from our sins in his own blood, and hath made us kings and priests unto God and his Father; to him be glory and dominion for ever and ever. Amen" (Revelation 1:5b-6).

10. What does Christ Jesus do as prophet?
He teaches us the way of salvation.

"I will raise them up a Prophet from among their brethren, like unto thee, and will put my words in his mouth; and he shall speak unto them all that I shall command him" (Deuteronomy 18:18).

"And I will bring the blind by a way that they knew not; I will lead them in paths that they have not known: I will make darkness light *before them, and crooked things straight. These things will I do unto them, and not forsake them"* (Isaiah 42:16).

11. *Why do we need Him as prophet?*

Because by nature we do not know the way back to God.

> *"There is none that understandeth, there is none that seeketh after God"* (Romans 3:11).

> *"Having the understanding darkened, being alienated from the life of God through the ignorance that is in them, because of the blindness of their heart"* (Ephesians 4:18).

12. *What did Christ do as priest?*

Jesus is the great High Priest, who offered Himself as a sacrifice for sin.

> *"For by one offering he hath perfected for ever them that are sanctified"* (Hebrews 10:14).

> *"How much more shall the blood of Christ, who through the eternal Spirit offered himself without spot to God, purge your conscience from dead works to serve the living God?"* (Hebrews 9:14).

13. *Why do I need Jesus as priest?*

To pay for my sin.

> *"And ye know that he was manifested to take away our sins; and in him is no sin"* (1 John 3:5).

> *"And he was numbered with the transgressors: and he bare the sin of many, and made intercession for the transgressors"* (Isaiah 53:12b).

14. What does Jesus do now as priest?

He makes intercession for His people.

> *"Who is he that condemneth? It is Christ that died, yea rather, that is risen again, who is even at the right hand of God, who also maketh intercession for us"* (Romans 8:34).

> *"My little children, these things write I unto you, that ye sin not. And if any man sin, we have an advocate with the Father, Jesus Christ the righteous"* (1 John 2:1).

15. What does intercession mean?

It means that Jesus continually shows the Father His sacrifice and prays for His children to be saved and preserved.

> *"I pray for them: I pray not for the world, but for them which thou hast given me; for they are thine"* (John 17:9).

> *"Father, I will that they also, whom thou hast given me, be with me where I am; that they may behold my glory, which thou hast given me: for thou lovedst me before the foundation of the world"* (John 17:24).

16. What does Jesus do as king?

He rules over all things and protects His people.

> *"And Jesus came and spake unto them, saying, All power is given unto me in heaven and in earth"* (Matthew 28:18).

> *"Behold, the days come, saith the LORD, that I*

will raise unto David a righteous Branch, and a King shall reign and prosper, and shall execute judgment and justice in the earth" (Jeremiah 23:5).

17. *Why do I need Him as king?*

Because I need Him to fight for me against sin and the devil.

> *"The angel of the LORD encampeth round about them that fear him, and delivereth them"* (Psalm 34:7).

> *"For the eyes of the LORD run to and fro throughout the whole earth, to shew himself strong in the behalf of them whose heart is perfect toward him"* (2 Chronicles 16:9).

18. *What does the Holy Spirit do for His people?*

He convicts them of sin, righteousness, and judgment (John 16:8), and guides them in the way of salvation.

> *"Create in me a clean heart, O God; and renew a right spirit within me. Cast me not away from thy presence; and take not thy holy spirit from me"* (Psalm 51:10-11).

> *"Howbeit when he, the Spirit of truth, is come, he will guide you into all truth"* (John 16:13a).

19. *What else does He do?*

He comforts the believer by revealing to him the Lord Jesus Christ.

> *"But when the Comforter is come, whom I will send unto you from the Father, even the Spirit of*

truth, which proceedeth from the Father, he shall testify of me" (John 15:26).

"And I will pray the Father, and he shall give you another Comforter, that he may abide with you for ever; even the Spirit of truth; whom the world cannot receive, because it seeth him not, neither knoweth him: but ye know him; for he dwelleth with you, and shall be in you. I will not leave you comfortless: I will come to you" (John 14:16-18).

20. What is sanctification?

It is the work of the Holy Spirit continuously turning the believer from sin to God.

"And I will put my spirit within you, and cause you to walk in my statutes, and ye shall keep my judgments and do them" (Ezekiel 36: 27).

"Elect according to the foreknowledge of God the Father, through sanctification of the Spirit, unto obedience and sprinkling of the blood of Jesus Christ" (1 Peter 1:2a).

21. What is it to be sanctified, or to be made holy?

It means that every day we repent of our sins, flee to Jesus Christ for forgiveness, and live thankfully unto God's glory.

"But there is forgiveness with thee, that thou mayest be feared" (Psalm 130:4).

"Knowing this, that our old man is crucified with him, that the body of sin might be destroyed, that henceforth we should not serve sin" (Romans 6:6).

22. *Why do we need the work of the Holy Spirit in our hearts?*

Without the Holy Spirit to teach and guide us, we would never come to Christ or live to God's glory.

> *"Jesus answered, Verily, verily, I say unto thee, Except a man be born of water and of the Spirit, he cannot enter into the kingdom of God"* (John 3:5).

> *"Likewise the Spirit also helpeth our infirmities: for we know not what we should pray for as we ought: but the Spirit itself maketh intercession for us with groanings which cannot be uttered"* (Romans 8:26).

Questions to think about:

1. Do you believe that the Lord earnestly invites you to salvation and commands you to repent and believe the gospel?

2. Why do you need the Lord Jesus Christ as prophet, priest, and king?

3. Do you ask Jesus to intercede for you?

4. Do you ask the Holy Spirit to live and work in your heart?

5. Are you sorry for your sins? Do you turn from your sins to God?

6. How can Jesus' blood cleanse you from all your sins?

7. Do you long to be holy? If so, why?

CHAPTER SIX
The Church and the Sacraments

1. *What is the true church?*
   The true church is the children of God and
   the body of Christ.

   > *"And the Lord added to the church daily such as
   > should be saved"* (Acts 2:47b).

   > *"And I say also unto thee, That thou art Peter,
   > and upon this rock I will build my church; and
   > the gates of hell shall not prevail against it"*
   > (Matthew 16:18).

2. *Who is the head of the church?*
   Christ is the head of the church.

   > *"For the husband is the head of the wife, even as
   > Christ is the head of the church"* (Ephesians
   > 5:23a).

   > *"And he is the head of the body, the church"*
   > (Colossians 1:18).

3. *Who are the living members of this church?*
   God's children, all of whom believe in Christ
   alone for salvation.

   > *"For no man ever yet hated his own flesh; but*

nourisheth and cherisheth it, even as the Lord the church: for we are members of his body, of his flesh, and of his bones" (Ephesians 5:29-30).

"Take heed therefore unto yourselves, and to all the flock, over the which the Holy Ghost hath made you overseers, to feed the church of God, which he hath purchased with his own blood" (Acts 20:28).

4. *Are God's children who have died also the church of God?*

Yes, they are called the church triumphant because they have been given the victory.

"To him that overcometh will I grant to sit with me in my throne, even as I also overcame, and am set down with my Father in his throne" (Revelation 3:21).

"To him that overcometh will I give to eat of the tree of life, which is in the midst of the paradise of God" (Revelation 2:7b).

5. *What do God's children fight against?*

Against sin, self, and Satan.

"But I see another law in my members, warring against the law of my mind, and bringing me into captivity to the law of sin which is in my members" (Romans 7:23).

"Be sober, be vigilant; because your adversary the devil, as a roaring lion, walketh about, seeking whom he may devour" (1 Peter 5:8).

6. *What is the church on earth called?*

It is called the church militant because it is still fighting this battle.

"Fight the good fight of faith, lay hold on eternal life" (1 Timothy 6:12a).

"Put on the whole armour of God, that ye may be able to stand against the wiles of the devil. For we wrestle not against flesh and blood, but against principalities, against powers, against the rulers of the darkness of this world, against spiritual wickedness in high places" (Ephesians 6:11-12).

7. *Why must God's people go to God's house on the Sabbath?*
They go to hear the preaching of God's Word, use the sacraments, pray, and worship God.

"And he came to Nazareth, where he had been brought up: and, as his custom was, he went into the synagogue on the sabbath day, and stood up for to read" (Luke 4:16).

"And many nations shall come, and say, Come, and let us go up to the mountain of the LORD, and to the house of the God of Jacob; and he will teach us of his ways, and we will walk in his paths: for the law shall go forth of Zion, and the word of the LORD from Jerusalem" (Micah 4:2).

8. *Are all people who go to church God's children?*
No, only those who are in Christ by faith.

"For ye are all the children of God by faith in Christ Jesus" (Galatians 3:26).

"But of him are ye in Christ Jesus, who of God

is made unto us wisdom, and righteousness, and sanctification, and redemption" (1 Corinthians 1:30).

9. What is a sacrament?

It is a holy, visible sign and seal of God's promises.

"And ye shall circumcise the flesh of your foreskin; and it shall be a token of the covenant betwixt me and you" (Genesis 17:11).

"For as often as ye eat this bread, and drink this cup, ye do shew the Lord's death till he come" (1 Corinthians 11:26).

10. What are the two sacraments?

Holy baptism and the Lord's Supper.

"For the promise is unto you, and to your children, and to all that are afar off, even as many as the Lord our God shall call" (Acts 2:39).

"For as often as ye eat this bread, and drink this cup, ye do shew the Lord's death till he come" (1 Corinthians 11:26).

11. Who began, or instituted, these sacraments?

The Lord Jesus Christ.

"Teach all nations, baptizing them..." (Matthew 28:19a).

"And as they were eating, Jesus took bread, and blessed it, and brake it, and gave it to the disciples, and said, Take, eat; this is my body. And he took the cup, and gave thanks, and gave it to them, saying, Drink ye all of it; for this is my blood of the

new testament, which is shed for many for the remission of sins" (Matthew 26:26-28).

12. In whose name are we baptized?

In the name of the Father, the Son, and the Holy Ghost.

"Go ye therefore, and teach all nations, baptizing them in the name of the Father, and of the Son, and of the Holy Ghost" (Matthew 28:19).

13. For what purpose were sacraments given?

God gave the sacraments to strengthen the faith of His people and to help us better understand the gospel.

"And now why tarriest thou? arise, and be baptized, and wash away thy sins, calling on the name of the Lord" (Acts 22:16).

"For my flesh is meat indeed, and my blood is drink indeed. He that eateth my flesh, and drinketh my blood, dwelleth in me, and I in him" (John 6:55-56).

14. What is the gospel?

The gospel is the good news that God, because of the Lord Jesus Christ's sacrifice on the cross, graciously gives forgiveness of sin and eternal life to unworthy sinners who believe in His Son.

"For this is my blood of the new testament, which is shed for many for the remission of sins" (Matthew 26:28).

"This is a faithful saying, and worthy of all

acceptation, that Christ Jesus came into the world to save sinners; of whom I am chief" (1 Timothy 1:15).

15. What does God promise in baptism?

That just as dirt is washed away by water, so Christ Jesus promises to wash away the sins of people who repent and believe in Him.

> *"But there is forgiveness with thee, that thou mayest be feared"* (Psalm 130:4).

> *"Who is a God like unto thee, that pardoneth iniquity, and passeth by the transgression of the remnant of his heritage? he retaineth not his anger for ever, because he delighteth in mercy"* (Micah 7:18).

16. Does the water of baptism actually wash away our sin?

No; only the blood of Jesus Christ can save us.

> *"The blood of Jesus Christ his Son cleanseth us from all sin"* (1 John 1:7b).

> *"Unto him that loved us, and washed us from our sins in his own blood"* (Revelation 1:5b).

17. How does baptism help me?

I may use these precious promises as a pleading ground before God for His covenant blessings in Christ.

> *"I love them that love me; and those that seek me early shall find me"* (Proverbs 8:17).

> *"Grace and peace be multiplied unto you*

through the knowledge of God, and of Jesus our Lord,...whereby are given unto us exceeding great and precious promises ..." (2 Peter 1:2, 4a).

18. *What is the pleading ground in baptism?*
It is God's promise, given to me by God Himself, that He will save children of believers.

> "But Jesus said, Suffer little children, and forbid them not, to come unto me: for of such is the kingdom of heaven. And he laid his hands on them" (Matthew 19:14, 15a).

> "And the Spirit and the bride say, Come. And let him that heareth say, Come. And whosoever will, let him take the water of life freely" (Revelation 22:17).

19. *Should infants also be baptized?*
Yes, for they are also included in God's covenant promise.

> "For the promise is unto you, and to your children, and to all that are afar off, even as many as the Lord our God shall call" (Acts 2:39).

> "And I will establish my covenant between me and thee and thy seed after thee in their generations for an everlasting covenant, to be a God unto thee, and to thy seed after thee" (Genesis 17:7).

20. *How are baptized children different from children who have not been baptized?*
They belong to the church and to God

because God has made a covenant with them.

"For the unbelieving husband is sanctified by the wife, and the unbelieving wife is sanctified by the husband: else were your children unclean; but now are they holy" (1 Corinthians 7:14).

"I was cast upon thee from the womb: thou art my God from my mother's belly" (Psalm 22:10).

21. What does God show to us in baptism?
That He is sincere, merciful, and faithful when He offers us the forgiveness of our sin.

"The Lord is not slack concerning his promise, as some men count slackness; but is longsuffering to us-ward, not willing that any should perish, but that all should come to repentance" (2 Peter 3:9).

"If ye then, being evil, know how to give good gifts unto your children: how much more shall your heavenly Father give the Holy Spirit to them that ask him?" (Luke 11:13).

22. What must I learn from God's sincere offers of mercy?
That I must not abuse nor neglect God's mercy, but flee today to the Lord Jesus Christ.

"Wherefore, as the Holy Ghost saith, Today if ye will hear his voice, harden not your hearts" (Hebrews 3:7-8a).

"For he saith, I have heard thee in a time

accepted, and in the day of salvation have I succoured thee: behold, now is the accepted time; behold, now is the day of salvation" (2 Corinthians 6:2).

23. What two things are present at the Lord's Supper?
Broken bread and the cup of wine.

> *"And he took bread, and gave thanks, and brake it, and gave unto them, saying, This is my body which is given for you: this do in remembrance of me. Likewise also the cup after supper, saying, This cup is the new testament in my blood, which is shed for you"* (Luke 22:19-20).

24. What does the bread represent?
The broken bread points to the broken body of Christ.

> *"That the Lord Jesus the same night in which he was betrayed took bread: and when he had given thanks, he brake it, and said, Take, eat: this is my body, which is broken for you: this do in re-membrance of me"* (1 Corinthians 11:23b-24).

25. What does the cup of wine represent?
The wine represents Christ's blood.

> *"After the same manner also he took the cup, when he had supped, saying, This cup is the new testament in my blood: this do ye, as oft as ye drink it, in remembrance of me"* (1 Corinthians 11:25).

26. Who may attend the Lord's Supper?
True believers who have publicly confessed

faith in Christ and are not willingly living in sin.

> *"He that eateth my flesh, and drinketh my blood, dwelleth in me, and I in him"* (John 6:56).

> *"But let a man examine himself, and so let him eat of that bread, and drink of that cup"* (1 Corinthians 11:28).

27. *What has God commanded His people to do at the Lord's Supper?*
They must remember Jesus Christ and His precious sacrifice for them as they eat the bread and drink the wine, and feed on Him in their hearts by faith.

> *"This do in remembrance of me"* (1 Corinthians 11:24b).

> *"For as often as ye eat this bread, and drink this cup, ye do shew the Lord's death till he come"* (1 Corinthians 11:26).

28. *Why must believers remember the suffering and death of Jesus Christ at the Lord's Supper?*
Because by His broken body and shed blood He saved them.

> *"The blood of Jesus Christ his Son cleanseth us from all sin"* (1 John 1:7b).

> *"Much more then, being now justified by his blood, we shall be saved from wrath through him"* (Romans 5:9).

29. *What is the purpose of the Lord's Supper?*

To strengthen the faith of believers by assuring them that Jesus has paid for their sin on the cross and that He loves them, and by nourishing their souls unto everlasting life.

> *"Likewise also the cup after supper, saying, This cup is the new testament in my blood, which is shed for you"* (Luke 22:20).

> *"That the Lord Jesus the same night in which he was betrayed took bread: and when he had given thanks, he brake it, and said, Take, eat: this is my body, which is broken for you: this do in remembrance of me"* (1 Corinthians 11:23b-24).

30. *How must church members prepare to attend the Lord's Supper?*

They must be truly humbled for their sins, believe in Jesus Christ alone for their salvation, and desire to live a holy life.

> *"Blessed are the poor in spirit: for theirs is the kingdom of heaven. . . . Blessed are they which do hunger and thirst after righteousness: for they shall be filled"* (Matthew 5:3, 6).

> *"What shall I render unto the LORD for all his benefits toward me? I will take the cup of salvation, and call upon the name of the LORD. I will pay my vows unto the LORD now in the presence of all his people"* (Psalm 116:12-14).

Questions to think about:

1. Do you belong to the church of God? Do you love the people of God?

2. Do you ask the Lord for a new heart that hates sin and fights against it?

3. Do you like to go to church, or do you complain about having to go to church? How should you ask the Lord to bless the preaching of God's Word to your heart?

4. How can you use your baptism as a pleading ground for God's covenant blessings in Christ?

5. Do you want to be washed in the blood of Christ? Do you feel the need of it?

CHAPTER SEVEN

Heaven and Hell

1. What is the punishment for sin?
Death.

> *"For the wages of sin is death"* (Romans 6:23a).
>
> *"The soul that sinneth, it shall die"* (Ezekiel 18:4b).

2. What happens to your body when you die?
It returns to dust, from which we were formed.

> *"In the sweat of thy face shalt thou eat bread, till thou return unto the ground; for out of it wast thou taken: for dust thou art, and unto dust shalt thou return"* (Genesis 3:19).
>
> *"All flesh shall perish together, and man shall turn again unto dust"* (Job 34:15).

3. Is your body destroyed forever?
No, God will raise it up at the last day.

> *"For this corruptible must put on incorruption, and this mortal must put on immortality"* (1 Corinthians 15:53).
>
> *"There shall be a resurrection of the dead, both of the just and the unjust"* (Acts 24:15).

4. Will there be a difference between the bodies of believers and those of unbelievers?

The bodies of believers will be made perfect, like Christ, but the bodies of unbelievers will be cast into hell.

> *"For our conversation is in heaven; from whence also we look for the Saviour, the Lord Jesus Christ: who shall change our vile body, that it may be fashioned like unto his glorious body"* (Philippians 3:20-21a).

> *"And as we have borne the image of the earthy, we shall also bear the image of the heavenly"* (1 Corinthians 15:49).

5. What happens to your soul when you die?

My soul will go immediately to God, who will bring my soul to heaven or send it to hell.

> *"Then shall the dust return to the earth as it was: and the spirit shall return unto God who gave it"* (Ecclesiastes 12:7).

> *"And Jesus said unto him, Verily I say unto thee, To day shalt thou be with me in paradise"* (Luke 23:43).

6. What is heaven?

God's home.

> *"Unto thee lift I up mine eyes, O thou that dwellest in the heavens"* (Psalm 123:1).

> *"And hear thou in heaven thy dwelling place: and when thou hearest, forgive"* (1 Kings 8:30b).

7. *Why is heaven so wonderful for God's children?*
Because their Savior is there.

> *"For I am in a strait betwixt two, having a desire to depart, and be with Christ; which is far better"* (Philippians 1:23).

> *"Father, I will that they also, whom thou hast given me, be with me where I am; that they may behold my glory, which thou hast given me: for thou lovedst me before the foundation of the world"* (John 17:24).

8. *What is hell?*
A place where God pours out His just fury against unbelieving and ungodly sinners.

> *"He that believeth and is baptized shall be saved; but he that believeth not shall be damned"* (Mark 16:16).

> *"The wicked shall be turned into hell, and all the nations that forget God"* (Psalm 9:17).

9. *Why is hell so terrible?*
Because God is there only in His holy anger.

> *"Then shall he say unto them on the left hand, Depart from me, ye cursed, into everlasting fire, prepared for the devil and his angels"* (Matthew 25:41).

> *"He that believeth on the Son hath everlasting life: and he that believeth not the Son shall not see life; but the wrath of God abideth on him"* (John 3:36).

10. *What will happen when Jesus returns on the clouds?*
The final judgment.

> *"For the Son of man shall come in the glory of his Father with his angels; and then he shall reward every man according to his works"* (Matthew 16:27).

> *"When the Son of man shall come in his glory, and all the holy angels with him, then shall he sit upon the throne of his glory: and before him shall be gathered all nations: and he shall separate them one from another, as a shepherd divideth his sheep from the goats"* (Matthew 25:31-32).

11. *What will happen to those people who are still living when Jesus comes back on the clouds?*
They will rise to meet Him, and their bodies will immediately be changed.

> *"For the Lord himself shall descend from heaven with a shout, with the voice of the archangel, and with the trump of God: and the dead in Christ shall rise first: then we which are alive and remain shall be caught up together with them in the clouds, to meet the Lord in the air: and so shall we ever be with the Lord"* (1 Thessalonians 4:16-17).

> *"Behold, I show you a mystery; We shall not all sleep, but we shall all be changed, in a moment, in the twinkling of an eye, at the last trump: for the trumpet shall sound, and the dead shall be raised incorruptible, and we shall be changed"* (1 Corinthians 15:51-52).

12. *Who will be the Judge?*
   The Lord Jesus Christ.

   > *"For we shall all stand before the judgment seat of Christ"* (Romans 14:10b).

   > *"For the Father judgeth no man, but hath committed all judgment unto the Son"* (John 5:22).

13. *Does anyone know when this will happen?*
   No one knows, not even the angels, but we must always be ready.

   > *"Be ye therefore ready also: for the Son of man cometh at an hour when ye think not"* (Luke 12:40).

   > *"But of that day and that hour knoweth no man, no, not the angels which are in heaven, neither the Son, but the Father. Take ye heed, watch and pray: for ye know not when the time is"* (Mark 13:32-33).

14. *Who will be judged?*
   All people.

   > *"And before him shall be gathered all nations: and he shall separate them one from another, as a shepherd divideth his sheep from the goats"* (Matthew 25:32).

   > *"For we must all appear before the judgment seat of Christ"* (2 Corinthians 5:10b).

15. *What will Jesus say to the unbelievers, the "goats"?*
   "Depart from me, ye cursed, into everlasting fire, prepared for the devil and his angels" (Matthew 25:41).

"And then will I profess unto them, I never knew you: depart from me, ye that work iniquity" (Matthew 7:23).

16. *Will there be people who have lived outwardly as Christians in this group?*
Sadly, yes. Unless we put our trust in Jesus Christ alone, we will be lost.

> *"But the children of the kingdom shall be cast out into outer darkness: there shall be weeping and gnashing of teeth"* (Matthew 8:12).

> *"For they are not all Israel, which are of Israel"* (Romans 9:6b).

17. *What will Jesus say to the believers, the "sheep"?*
"Come, ye blessed of my Father, inherit the kingdom prepared for you from the foundation of the world" (Matthew 25:34).

> *"In my Father's house are many mansions: if it were not so, I would have told you. I go to prepare a place for you. And if I go and prepare a place for you, I will come again, and receive you unto myself; that where I am, there ye may be also"* (John 14:2-3).

18. *How long will people stay in heaven or in hell?*
Forever and ever; for eternity.

> *"And these shall go away into everlasting punishment: but the righteous into life eternal"* (Matthew 25:46).

> *"And many of them that sleep in the dust of the*

earth shall awake, some to everlasting life, and some to shame and everlasting contempt" (Daniel 12:2).

19. *Do only very wicked people go to hell?*

All those who are not born again, who do not trust, love, and serve the Lord Jesus Christ with all their hearts, will go to hell.

> *"For I say unto you, That except your righteousness shall exceed the righteousness of the scribes and Pharisees, ye shall in no case enter into the kingdom of heaven"* (Matthew 5:20).

> *"Jesus answered and said unto him, Verily, verily, I say unto thee, Except a man be born again, he cannot see the kingdom of God"* (John 3:3).

20. *Do people who have lived a decent, respectable life go to heaven?*

Only if their hearts have been cleansed and renewed in the blood of Christ.

> *"Verily I say unto you, Except ye be converted, and become as little children, ye shall not enter into the kingdom of heaven"* (Matthew 18:3).

> *"And such were some of you: but ye are washed, but ye are sanctified, but ye are justified in the name of the Lord Jesus, and by the Spirit of our God"* (1 Corinthians 6:11).

21. *What must I do to receive eternal life?*

We must repent before God and "believe on the Lord Jesus Christ," put our trust in Him, and walk in His ways.

"And they said, Believe on the Lord Jesus Christ, and thou shalt be saved, and thy house" (Acts 16:31).

"I am come a light into the world, that whosoever believeth on me should not abide in darkness" (John 12:46).

22. *Will Jesus ever turn me away if I truly ask Him for a new heart?*

Never, for the Savior Himself said, "Him that cometh to me I will in no wise cast out" (John 6:37b).

"For whosoever shall call upon the name of the Lord shall be saved" (Romans 10:13).

"And I say unto you, Ask, and it shall be given you; seek, and ye shall find; knock, and it shall be opened unto you. For every one that asketh receiveth; and he that seeketh findeth; and to him that knocketh it shall be opened" (Luke 11:9-10).

Questions to think about:

1. What will Jesus say to you when He returns?

2. Why should you think about the day of your death? Are you ready to die?

3. Do you desire to live with Jesus forever?

4. Do you want to serve God by walking in His ways?

Notes

Notes

Building on the Rock Books 1-5

Look out for this new series of devotional books for young people by Joel Beeke and Diana Kleyn

152 stories
with Scripture readings and other bible verses to investigate.
Line art illustrations included.
All scripture taken from King James Version of the Bible.
Questions to answer and discussion starters.
Prayer points to use and think over during personal and family devotional times

Book 1
How God used
a Thunderstorm
Book 2
How God stopped
the Pirates
Book 3
How God used
a Snowdrift
Book 4
How God used a Drought
and an Umbrella
Book 5
How God sent a dog
to save a family

Other books published by
Christian Focus Publications in
connection with Reformation
Heritage Books.

A first
Catechism by
Carine
Mackenzie and
Teacher's
Manual by
Diana Kleyn

Doctrines and subjects covered in
these two titles include:

God
Creation
How man sinned
What happened
because of sin
Salvation
Jesus as Prophet,
Priest and King
The Ten Commandments
Keeping God's Laws
The way to be Saved
Experiencing God's Salvation
Baptism and
the Lord's Supper
Prayer
Where is Jesus now?
Death
Hell
Heaven

CHRISTIAN FOCUS

Staying Faithful. Reaching Out.

Christian Focus Publications publishes biblically-accurate books for adults and children. If you are looking for quality Bible teaching for children then we have a wide and excellent range of Bible story books - from board books to teenage fiction, we have it covered. There are also children's catechisms and teachers manuals available - excellent resources for Sunday school teachers and pastors. Our aim is to help children find out about God and get them enthusiastic about reading the Bible, now and later in their lives.

www.christianfocus.com

Reformation Heritage Books

2919 Leonard St, NE, Grand Rapids, MI, 49525
Phone: 616-977-0599 Fax: 616-285-3246
email: RHBookstore@aol.com
Website: www.heritagebooks.org

Reformation Heritage Books, Inc. is a non-profit organization, formed for the sole purpose of disseminating sound Christian literature world-wide. All proceeds from the sale of books are returned to the fund for the publication of Reformed material.